This book is presented to:

_____

Little Bible Heroes™
Storybook

↑

For added fun and learning, each story includes a QR code that links to a corresponding video. Just scan the code with any QR code-reader app to start the fun.

ISBN: 978-1-4336-9230-7

Dewey Decimal Classification: CE
Subject Heading: HEROES AND HEROINES—FICTION \
BIBLE STORIES \ COURAGE—FICTION

Scripture references are taken from the Holman Christian Standard Bible ®
Copyright © 1999, 2000, 2002, 2003, 2009 by Holman Bible Publishers.
Used by permission.

Printed in Huizhou, Guangdong, China, May 2016

1 2 3 4 5 6 7 8 20 19 18 17 16

Little Bible Heroes™
Storybook

GOLDQUILL
WWW.GOLDQUILL.CO.UK

B&H
KIDS
NASHVILLE, TENNESSEE

Contents

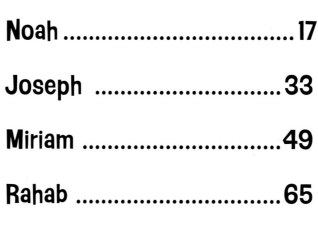

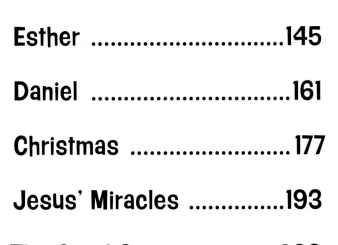

Little Bible Heroes™
Creation

Written by Victoria Kovacs
Illustrated by Mike Krome

Scan for a video of the story!

In the beginning, God created everything. On the first day, He said, "Let there be light." On the second day, God made the sky.

On the third day, God made the oceans and the land. He also made the grass and plants and trees to grow.

On the fourth day,
God made the sun
and moon and stars.

On the fifth day, God made birds and all the creatures that live in the sea.

9

On the sixth day, God made all the animals on the earth. He also made Adam and Eve, the first people.

God looked at what He had made.
It was a good new world.

On the seventh day, God rested from all His work. His creation was finished!

Read:
In the beginning God created the heavens and the earth.—Genesis 1:1

Think:
1. God created the whole world. What do you like to create?
2. What is your favorite thing that God made?

Remember:
The heavens are Yours; the earth also is Yours. The world and everything in it— You founded them.
—Psalm 89:11

Little Bible Heroes™
Noah

Written by Victoria Kovacs
Illustrated by Mike Krome

↑
Scan for a video of the story!

Noah is a righteous man and does what God says to do. But the other people on earth are bad. That makes God sad.

19

God tells Noah to build an ark. The ark is taller than a three-story building! Noah brings animals into the ark.

Once all the animals and Noah's family are in the ark, God makes it rain for forty days and nights.

Noah sends out a dove. The dove returns with an olive leaf. That means the water is finally going down!

Everyone on the ark is waiting and waiting. The ground will soon be dry.

Noah and his family and all the animals leave the ark. Noah builds an altar to God. He thanks God for saving their lives.

God puts the rainbow in the sky as His promise that He will never again flood the earth.

Read:

Then the LORD said to Noah, "Enter the ark, you and all your household, for I have seen that you alone are righteous before Me in this generation."—Genesis 7:1

Think:

1. Would you like being on the ark with Noah and the animals?
2. God always keeps His promises. Have you ever made a promise?

Remember:

"I will remember My covenant between Me and you and all the living creatures: water will never again become a flood to destroy every creature."
—Genesis 9:15

Little Bible Heroes™
Joseph

Written by Victoria Kovacs
Illustrated by Mike Krome

↑
Scan for a video of the story!

Joseph's father gives
Joseph a special coat.
His brothers are jealous.

The brothers want to get rid of Joseph. They sell him to a merchant going far away. They lie and tell their father that Joseph has died.

Joseph is put in prison in Egypt. Pharaoh is the ruler of Egypt. He finds out that Joseph can interpret dreams and tell what they mean.

God helps Joseph interpret Pharaoh's dreams. Pharaoh is so happy. He puts Joseph in charge of Egypt.

Joseph's brothers come to Egypt to buy food. Joseph forgives his brothers. He tells them that God sent him to Egypt to help people, including them.

All of Joseph's family moves to Egypt.
Joseph sees his father again.

45

Joseph is happy that God is always with him and brings his family back together.

47

Read:
Now Israel loved Joseph more than his other sons because Joseph was a son born to him in his old age, and he made a robe of many colors for him.—Genesis 37:3

Think:
1. How did God help Joseph?
2. Joseph forgave his brothers. Have you ever forgiven someone?

Remember:
God is always with us.

48

Little Bible Heroes™
Miriam

Written by Victoria Kovacs
Illustrated by Mike Krome

↑
Scan for a video of the story!

The ruler of Egypt is an evil pharaoh who orders all the Hebrew baby boys to be killed. One mother has a plan to protect her baby boy. She makes a papyrus basket, coats it with clay and tar to make it float, and places the baby inside.

The mother and her daughter, Miriam, put the basket in the reeds along the riverbank. They pray for God to take care of their baby.

53

Miriam is a very brave big sister. She hides and watches over her brother's floating basket.

Pharaoh's daughter comes to the river to take a bath. She sees the basket and looks inside.

Miriam is worried. What will the princess do to her little brother?

The princess picks up the basket and says, "I will take care of this baby as my own."

Miriam runs to the princess and asks bravely, "Would you like me to find a nurse for the baby?"

"Yes," answers the princess.

Miriam is happy. Now her brother is safe! She takes him home so their mother can be his nurse. The baby stays with his real family a little while longer.

When Miriam's brother is older, their mother brings him to the princess. The princess names him Moses. Moses grows up to become a great leader of his people.

Read:

When the child grew older, she brought him to Pharaoh's daughter, and he became her son. She named him Moses, "Because," she said, "I drew him out of the water."—Exodus 2:10

Think:

1. Has God ever protected you from trouble?
2. How was Miriam brave? When have you been brave?

Remember:

I will both lie down and sleep in peace, for You alone, LORD, make me live in safety.
—Psalm 4:8

Little Bible Heroes™
Rahab

Written by Victoria Kovacs
Illustrated by David Ryley

↑
Scan for a video of the story!

Rahab lives in Jericho. Jericho is a big city with tall, strong walls. God tells the army of Israel to conquer the land where Jericho stands.

Two spies from Israel enter the city. They need a place to hide from Jericho's soldiers. Rahab bravely hides the spies on her roof.

Rahab tricks the soldiers by telling them the spies left the city.

70

71

Rahab then lowers the spies out the window so they can escape.

The spies tell Rahab to hang a scarlet cord from her window and gather all her family into her house. If she does, her family will be safe when Israel's army arrives.

When the army captures the city, the spies see the scarlet cord and know which house belongs to Rahab. She and her family are safe!

Rahab's bravery saves her family. She goes on to become the great-great-great grandmother of another brave hero, King David.

Read:

Then she let them down by a rope through the window, since she lived in a house that was built into the wall of the city.
—Joshua 2:15

Think:

1. What do you think the city of Jericho was like?
2. Rahab is remembered for her good deed. Have you ever done a good deed?

Remember:

God wants us to help people, even when we must be brave to do so.

Little Bible Heroes™
Joshua

Written by Victoria Kovacs
Illustrated by David Ryley

↑
Scan for a video of the story!

God tells Joshua to lead the people of Israel into the Promised Land.

"Don't be afraid because I am with you," God says to Joshua.

Joshua sends two spies to explore the land and the great city of Jericho.

"Truly God has handed over all the land to us," the spies report. "The people of Jericho are terrified that we're coming."

The Israelites must cross the Jordan River to reach Jericho. When they carry the Ark of the Covenant into the river, God makes the river stop flowing! Everyone walks across on dry land.

Joshua takes twelve stones from the river to make an altar. The altar is to remind the people how powerful God is and to obey Him.

When the people reach Jericho, God tells them what to do. They obey. They march around the city for six days. On the seventh day, they march around the city seven times. The priests blow their horns. The people shout.

91

The walls of Jericho fall down flat!

Joshua was a great leader. He and his people obeyed God, and God gave them the Promised Land.

Read:

So the people shouted, and the trumpets sounded. When they heard the blast of the trumpet, the people gave a great shout, and the wall collapsed. The people advanced into the city, each man straight ahead, and they captured the city.—Joshua 6:20

Think:

1. How did Joshua obey God?
2. How do you obey God?

Remember:

God wants us to obey Him, no matter what.

Little Bible Heroes™
Samuel

Written by Victoria Kovacs
Illustrated by Mike Krome

Scan for a video of the story!

Hannah prays for a baby. God answers her prayers and gives her a baby boy named Samuel.

When Samuel is old enough, he goes to live in God's temple.

98

Samuel helps the high priest, Eli.
Samuel wears a special linen
vest that the priests wear. He is
a good boy and works hard.

One night, when Samuel is sleeping, he hears someone call his name. Samuel runs to Eli.

"Here I am. You called me?" Samuel says.

Eli yawns and shakes his head. "No, I didn't call you. Go back to bed."

Samuel hears someone call his name again. He runs to Eli, but the priest sends him back to bed.

Then Samuel hears someone call him a third time, so he runs and wakes up Eli once more.

105

"Here I am. You called me?"
Samuel says.

Eli knows that God is calling
Samuel. He tells Samuel, "If you
are called again, say, 'Speak, Lord.
Your servant is listening.'"

107

God calls Samuel again.

"Speak, Lord, your servant is listening," says Samuel.

God answers! This time, Samuel listens and hears an important message from God.

When he grows up, Samuel becomes a great prophet and leader. And he still listens to God.

Read:

The LORD came, stood there, and called as before, "Samuel, Samuel!" Samuel responded, "Speak, for Your servant is listening."
—1 Samuel 3:10

Think:

1. What do you think it was like for little Samuel to grow up in the temple?
2. God speaks to all of us in many ways. What are some ways God speaks to you?

Remember:

"The one who is from God listens to God's words."
—John 8:47

Little Bible Heroes™
David

Written by Victoria Kovacs
Illustrated by Mike Krome

↑
Scan for a video of the story!

David is a little shepherd boy.
He guards his father's sheep.

114

115

When a lion tries to take a lamb, David protects his sheep. He is very brave.

David takes food to his brothers, who are soldiers in Israel's army. The other army has a soldier named Goliath who is big and mean. Goliath challenges Israel's army to send out a soldier to fight him, but they are too afraid.

David isn't afraid. He tells the king, "God rescued me from a lion and a bear. He will rescue me from this giant."

David finds five smooth stones. He takes his slingshot and bravely faces Goliath.

"You're coming at me with a sword and a spear, but I'm coming at you in the name of God!" says David.

David slings a stone toward Goliath. Swoosh! The stone flies through the air and hits Goliath in the forehead. He falls to the ground. God has helped David defeat Goliath.

David the brave shepherd boy grows up to be David the king of Israel!

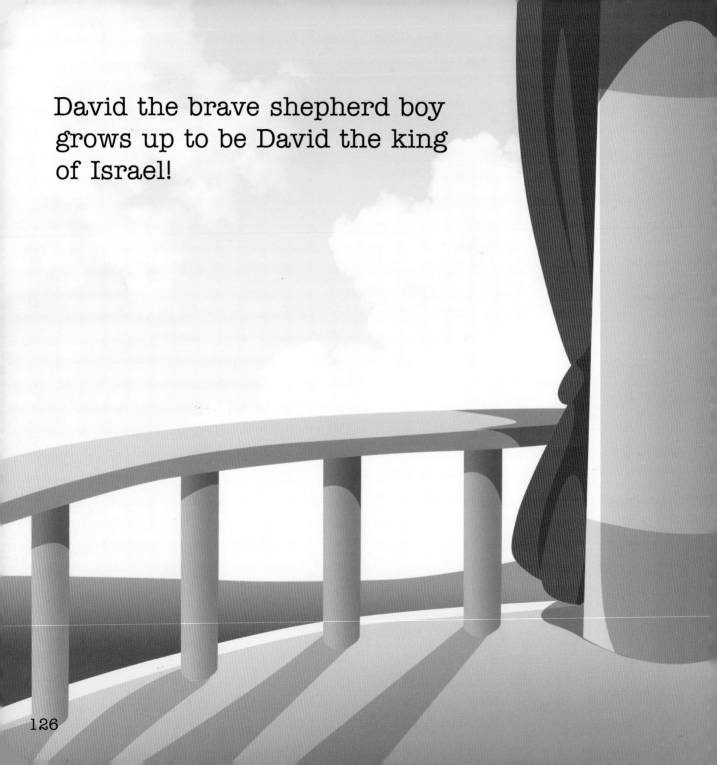

Read:

Then David said, "The LORD who rescued me from the paw of the lion and the paw of the bear will rescue me from the hand of this Philistine."—1 Samuel 17:37

Think:

1. Who is the bravest person you know?
2. Has God ever helped you do something brave?

Remember:

When we trust in God,
He can help us be brave!

Little Bible Heroes™
The Little Maid

Written by Victoria Kovacs
Illustrated by Mike Krome

Scan for a video of the story!

A warrior named Naaman is the commander of a big army. One day his army raids Israel and captures a little girl.

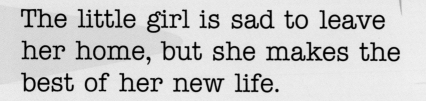

The little girl is sad to leave her home, but she makes the best of her new life.

She becomes a servant to Naaman's wife. The girl remembers her home and her God.

Naaman has a terrible sickness. The little servant girl tells him, "Elisha is God's prophet. He can heal you."

Naaman travels to Israel to see Elisha. Elisha says, "Wash in the Jordan River seven times, and you will be healed."

Naaman washes in the river.
His sickness is all gone!

Naaman is happy and knows that God has healed him.

Thanks to his little maid, Naaman is healed and learns about God's power.

143

Read:

Aram had gone on raids and brought back from the land of Israel a young girl who served Naaman's wife.—2 Kings 5:2

Think:

1. Who healed Naaman?
2. The little maid helped Naaman. How can you help people who are sick?

Remember:

"Worship the LORD your God, and He will bless your bread and your water. I will remove illnesses from you."
—Exodus 23:25

Little Bible Heroes™
Esther

Written by Victoria Kovacs
Illustrated by Mike Krome

↑
Scan for a video of the story!

The king of Babylon needs a new queen. He gathers all the beautiful girls in Babylon so he can choose one of them to be queen.

Esther is a Jewish girl who lives in Babylon. The king likes Esther best and picks her to be queen.

Haman is the king's helper. Haman hates Jews and tricks the king into killing them.

Esther gives a banquet for the king and Haman. The king likes the banquet so much that he says, "Esther, I'll give you anything you ask for."

Esther answers, "Haman wants to kill my people. Please stop him!"

The king is angry and stops Haman.

The Jewish people are
happy to be safe!

The holiday called Purim is still celebrated today to remember how Esther saved her people.

Read:

"If it pleases the king," Esther replied, "may the king and Haman come today to the banquet I have prepared for them."
—Esther 5:4

Think:

1. What would it be like to suddenly become a king or queen like Esther?
2. God uses His people to help others. How has God used you to help someone?

Remember:

God took care of Esther and her people, and He takes care of you too!

160

Little Bible Heroes™
Daniel

Written by Victoria Kovacs
Illustrated by David Ryley

↑
Scan for a video of the story!

Daniel is a young man in Israel.
When the king of Babylon conquers
the city of Jerusalem, he takes
Daniel and his friends to his palace
to work as his servants.

They are given unhealthy food and wine, but Daniel and his friends keep God's laws and choose vegetables and water instead. After ten days, they look healthier than the others and are allowed to keep obeying God's laws.

Later, the king has terrible dreams. He orders all the wise men put to death because they can't tell him what he dreamed and what the dreams mean.

"Nobody in the world can know your dreams and explain them!" the wise men plead.

Daniel is a wise man now too. He prays to God for help, and God tells him all about the king's dreams.

Daniel quickly goes to
the king and explains
what God had told him.
The king is very happy
to know what his dreams
mean.

The king now knows that Daniel's God is the one true God. To show his thanks, the king gives Daniel gifts and makes him a ruler over the country.

Years later, wicked men throw Daniel into a den of lions because he prayed to God instead of to the new king. God sends an angel to shut the lions' mouths. Daniel is saved!

Read:

Then the king promoted Daniel and gave him many generous gifts. He made him ruler over the entire province of Babylon and chief governor over all the wise men of Babylon.—Daniel 2:48

Think:

1. Is it hard to obey God when others tell you not to?
2. Daniel prayed to God for help. When has God answered your prayers and helped you?

Remember:

The LORD is far from the wicked, but He hears the prayer of the righteous.—Proverbs 15:29

Little Bible Heroes™

Christmas

Written by Victoria Kovacs
Illustrated by Mike Krome

↑
Scan for a video of the story!

The angel Gabriel appears to Mary. "You will have a Son, and you will name Him Jesus."

179

Mary visits her old cousin, Elizabeth. Elizabeth is going to have a baby too. Mary tells her, "The Mighty One has done great things for me!"

Mary and Joseph must travel
far away to Bethlehem.

There is no room for them at the inn, so Mary and Joseph go to a place where animals are kept. There Mary gives birth to Jesus on Christmas Day.

Shepherds see angels in the sky saying, "Glory to God!" An angel tells the shepherds that Jesus is born and lying in a manger.

187

The shepherds hurry to see Jesus.
They know Jesus is a special baby.

The wise men come from the east to worship Jesus. They give Him gold, frankincense, and myrrh.

191

Read:

Today a Savior, who is Messiah the Lord, was born for you in the city of David.
—Luke 2:11

Think:

1. Why is Christmas special?
2. What gifts can *you* give to Jesus?

Remember:

Thanks be to God for His indescribable gift.
—2 Corinthians 9:15

Little Bible Heroes™
Jesus' Miracles

Written by Victoria Kovacs
Illustrated by Mike Krome

↑
Scan for a video of the story!

What is a miracle? It is a supernatural act of God.

Jesus' first miracle was changing water into wine at a wedding.

Once Jesus and His followers were in a boat during a terrible storm. Jesus commanded the wind and the waves to be still, and they obeyed Him.

One day some friends lowered a paralyzed man through the roof to bring him to Jesus.

Jesus said, "Get up. Pick up your mat, and go home!" The man walked!

When Lazarus had been dead four days, Jesus came to his tomb. Jesus called, "Lazarus! Come out!"

Lazarus walked out. He was alive!

201

Jesus made five loaves and two fish into enough food to feed more than five thousand hungry people.

Jesus helped people everywhere He went. He helped the lame to walk and the blind to see.

The Bible tells us about dozens of miracles Jesus performed to help people. Isn't He amazing?

207

Read:
Jesus performed this first sign in Cana of Galilee. He displayed His glory, and His disciples believed in Him.—John 2:11

Think:
1. Which of Jesus' miracles is the most amazing to you?
2. Jesus helped a lot of people. How can you help people?

Remember:
Jesus can do amazing things, and He loves to help people.

Little Bible Heroes™
The Good Samaritan

Written by Victoria Kovacs
Illustrated by Mike Krome

↑
Scan for a video of the story!

Jesus tells His followers a story about the Good Samaritan. It is a story about loving your neighbor.

In the story, a Jew is traveling from Jerusalem to Jericho. Robbers attack him.

A priest goes down the same road.
When he sees the hurt man, he
doesn't stop to help.

A man who serves in God's temple sees the man. He doesn't stop to help either.

217

A Samaritan sees the man and stops to bandage his wounds. He puts the hurt man on his donkey and takes the man to an inn to care for him.

219

Samaritans and Jews usually don't like each other, but this Samaritan follows God's command to love his neighbor.

221

Jesus ends His story by telling us to love others just like the Good Samaritan did.

Read:
But a Samaritan on his journey came up to him, and when he saw the man, he had compassion.—Luke 10:33

Think:
1. Who is your neighbor?
2. How can you show love to your neighbor?

Remember:
Jesus loves us, and He wants us to show love to others too.

Little Bible Heroes™
Martha

Written by Victoria Kovacs
Illustrated by David Ryley

↑
Scan for a video of the story!

Jesus and His disciples went to a village called Bethany. A woman named Martha lived there. She invited Jesus to her house.

Martha had a sister named Mary. Mary sat at Jesus' feet listening to Him teach.

Martha was very busy doing all the work by herself. She was cooking and getting the house ready for Jesus.

Martha was upset that Mary was not helping with the work, so she complained to Jesus.

"Don't You care that my sister isn't helping me?" she asked.

Martha was surprised. Jesus gave a different answer than she thought He would give.

235

Jesus said, "Martha, Martha, you are worrying about so many things! But taking time to learn from Me is the most important thing."

Jesus wanted Martha to know that listening to Him is just as important as doing things for Him. Martha learned an important lesson!

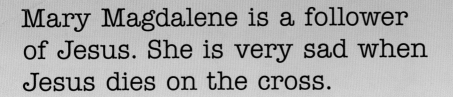

Mary Magdalene is a follower
of Jesus. She is very sad when
Jesus dies on the cross.

243

After Jesus is placed in a tomb,
Mary goes home to prepare spices
for His burial.

245

Three days later, Mary returns to the tomb, but it is empty. She sees an angel. He says, "Jesus is not here. He is risen!"

Mary tells Jesus' disciples about the empty tomb, but they don't believe her.

Mary goes back to the tomb, crying. She hears someone say her name. She sees Jesus!

Mary is so happy that Jesus is alive.

Jesus appears to His disciples.
He is risen!

255

Read:

"He is not here! For He has been resurrected, just as He said. Come and see the place where He lay."—Matthew 28:6

Think:

1. The day Jesus was resurrected is also called Easter. How do you celebrate Easter?
2. Why is Easter special?

Remember:

"For God loved the world in this way: He gave His One and Only Son, so that everyone who believes in Him will not perish but have eternal life." —John 3:16